RAY LAMONTAGNE TROUBLE

This publication is not authorised for sale in
the United States of America and/or Canada

Wise Publications
part of The Music Sales Group

London/New York/Paris/Sydney/Copenhagen/Berlin/Madrid/Tokyo

Published by
Wise Publications
14-15 Berners Street, London, W1T 3LJ, UK.

Exclusive distributors:
Music Sales Limited
Distribution Centre, Newmarket Road,
Bury St Edmunds, Suffolk, IP33 3YB, UK.

Music Sales Pty Limited
120 Rothschild Avenue, Rosebery,
NSW 2018, Australia.

Order No. AM990121
ISBN: 978-1-84772-032-0
This book © Copyright 2007 Wise Publications,
a division of Music Sales Limited.

Unauthorised reproduction of any part
of this publication by any means including
photocopying is an infringement of copyright.

Edited by Fiona Bolton.
Music arranged by Derek Jones.
Music processed by Paul Ewers Music Design.

Front cover painting by Jason Holley.
Original cover design by Cally (www.antar.cc).

Printed in the EU.

www.musicsales.com

Your Guarantee of Quality:
As publishers, we strive to produce every book
to the highest commercial standards.

Particular care has been given to specifying
acid-free, neutral-sized paper made from pulps
which have not been elemental chlorine bleached.

This pulp is from farmed sustainable forests
and was produced with special regard for the environment.

Throughout, the printing and binding have
been planned to ensure a sturdy, attractive
publication which should give years of enjoyment.

If your copy fails to meet our high standards,
please inform us and we will gladly replace it.

Trouble 4
Shelter 10
Hold You In My Arms 16
Narrow Escape 21
Burn 26
Forever My Friend 30
Hannah 40
How Come 35
Jolene 52
All The Wild Horses 46

Trouble

Words & Music by Ray LaMontagne

Shelter

Words & Music by Ray LaMontagne

Hold You In My Arms

Words & Music by Ray LaMontagne & Ethan Johns

Narrow Escape

Words & Music by Ray LaMontagne

© Copyright 2004 Sweet Mary Music, USA.
Chrysalis Music Limited.
All Rights Reserved. International Copyright Secured.

Burn

Words & Music by Ray LaMontagne

Ma - ma, don't walk a - way. I'm a god-
(2.) Ma - ma, don't leave me a - lone. With my
(3.) Ma - ma, don't walk a - way. You

© Copyright 2004 Sweet Mary Music, USA.
Chrysalis Music Limited.
All Rights Reserved. International Copyright Secured.

Forever My Friend

Words & Music by Ray LaMontagne

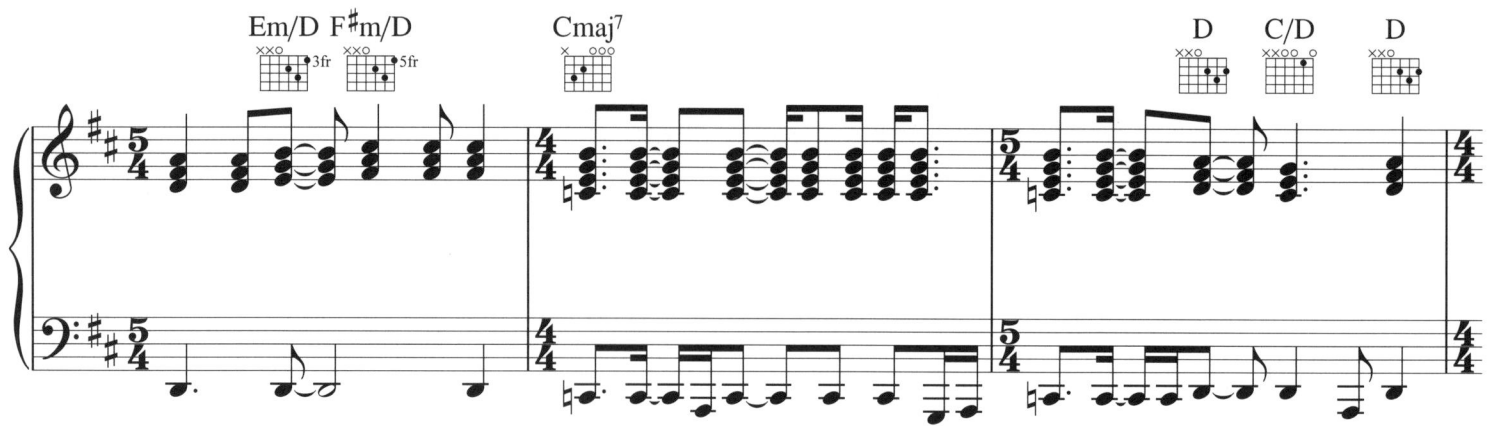

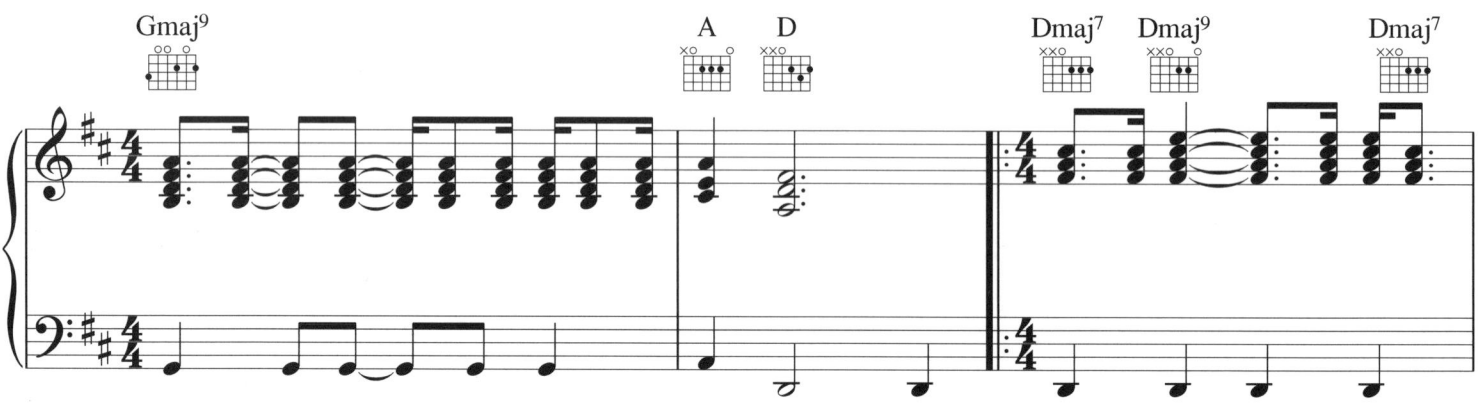
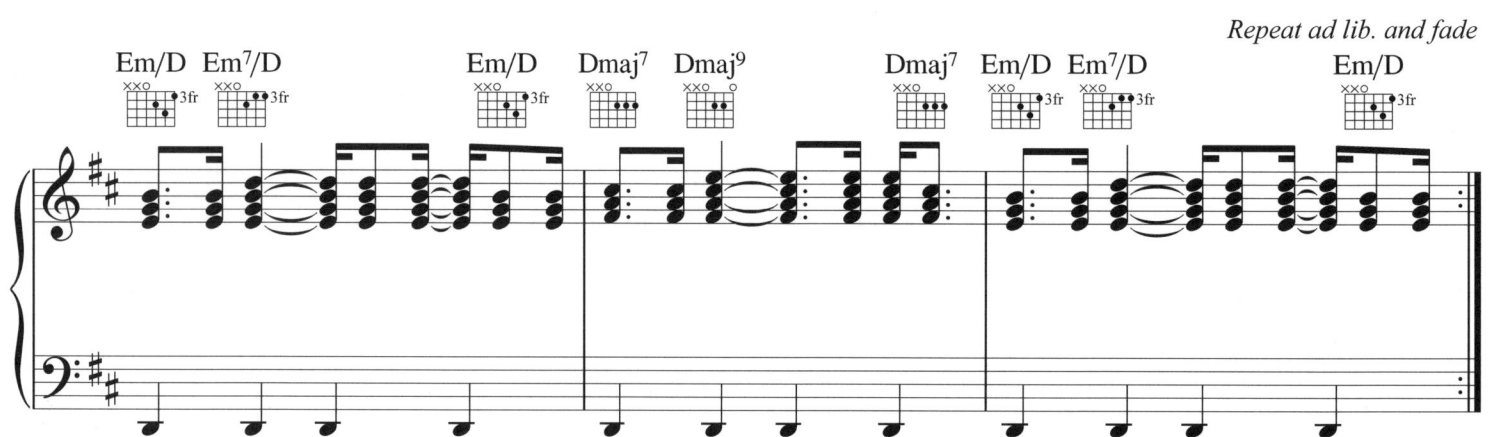

How Come

Words & Music by Ray LaMontagne

Hope-less-ness__ got some__ by the throat, you can see it in their eyes.__
Ev-'ry-bod-y try'n' to reach out to each oth-er but they don't know where to be-gin__
and free-dom can be an emp-ty cup from which ev-'ry-bod-y wan-na drink.__

1. I said how come?__

How come?__

2, 3. how come__ I can't tell__ the

free world___ from___ liv-ing hell?___ I said how___ come?___

How___ come___ all I see___ is a child of God in mis-er-y?___ I said how come?___

To Coda ⊕

D.C. al Coda

38

Coda
C
B♭
F
how come?
B♭ C C B♭
It's just man kill-ing man, kill-ing man,
F B♭ C
kill-ing man, kill-ing man. I don't un-der-stand it.
Repeat ad lib. and fade
B♭ F B♭ C
It's just

Hannah

Words & Music by Ray LaMontagne

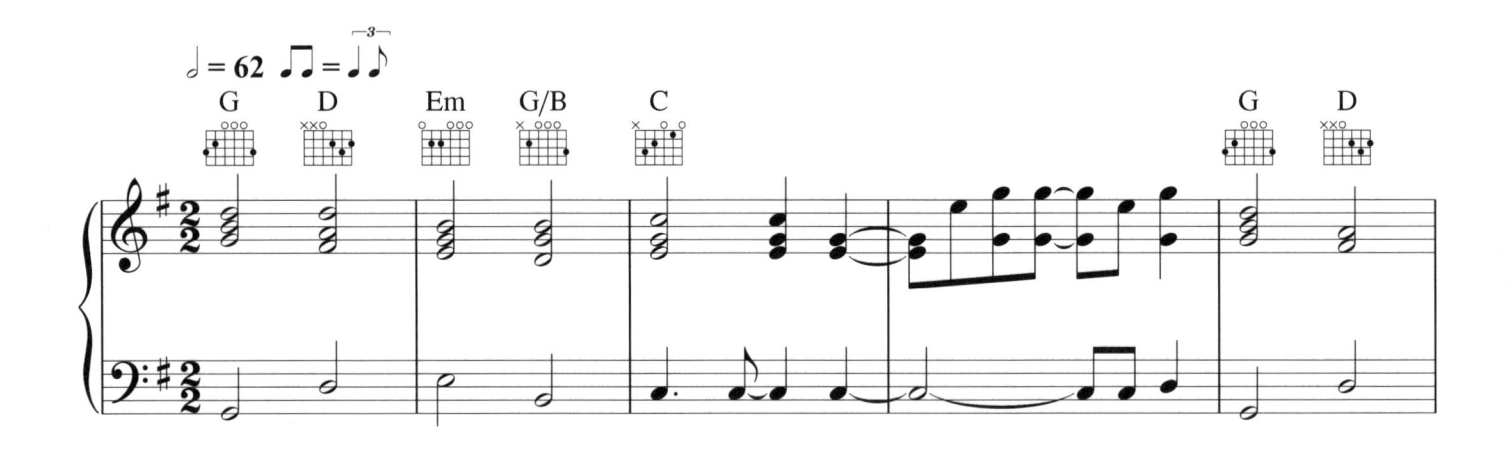

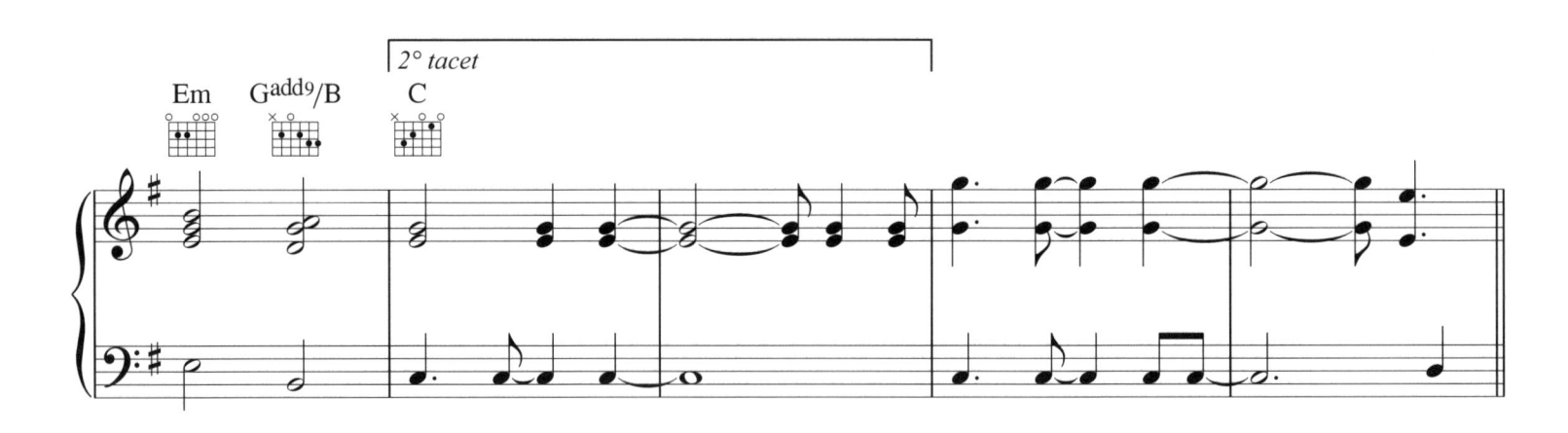

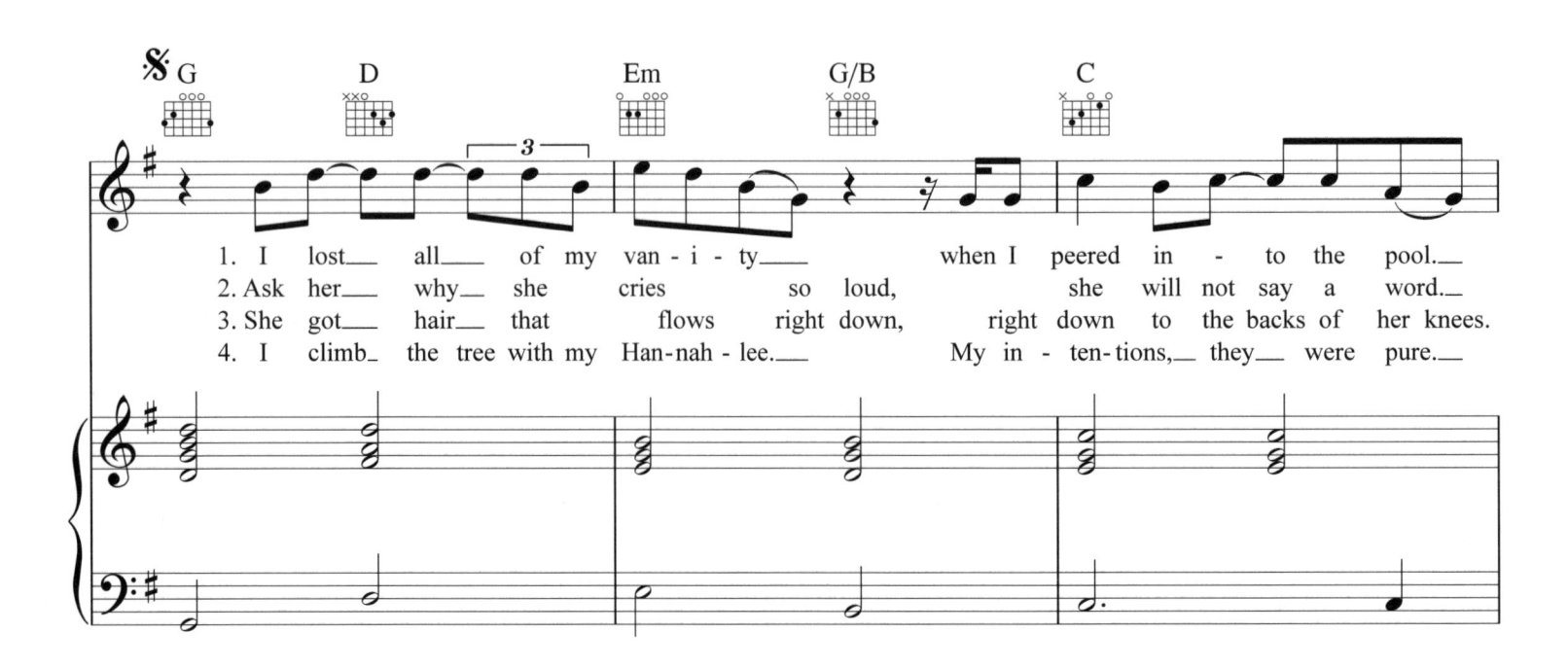

1. I lost all of my vanity when I peered into the pool.
2. Ask her why she cries so loud, she will not say a word.
3. She got hair that flows right down, right down to the backs of her knees.
4. I climb the tree with my Hannah-lee. My intentions, they were pure.

© Copyright 2004 Sweet Mary Music, USA.
Chrysalis Music Limited.
All Rights Reserved. International Copyright Secured.

I lost all of my in-no-cence when I
Eyes like ice and hands that shake, she
Her pa-pa, he was a preach-ing man and the
Oh, the breeze did whip and I lost my grip and I

fell in love with you. I nev-er knew a man could
takes what she de-serves. To cel-e-brate her
Lord is hard to please. So she comes down from the
tum-bled to-wards the earth. Yeah, you nev-er would guess who it was that

fall so far till I land-ed here. Where
emp-ti-ness in a cold and lone-ly room.
Oz-ark Hills to these ver-y streets to roam, with a
stood be-low. His name I will nev-er tell. His

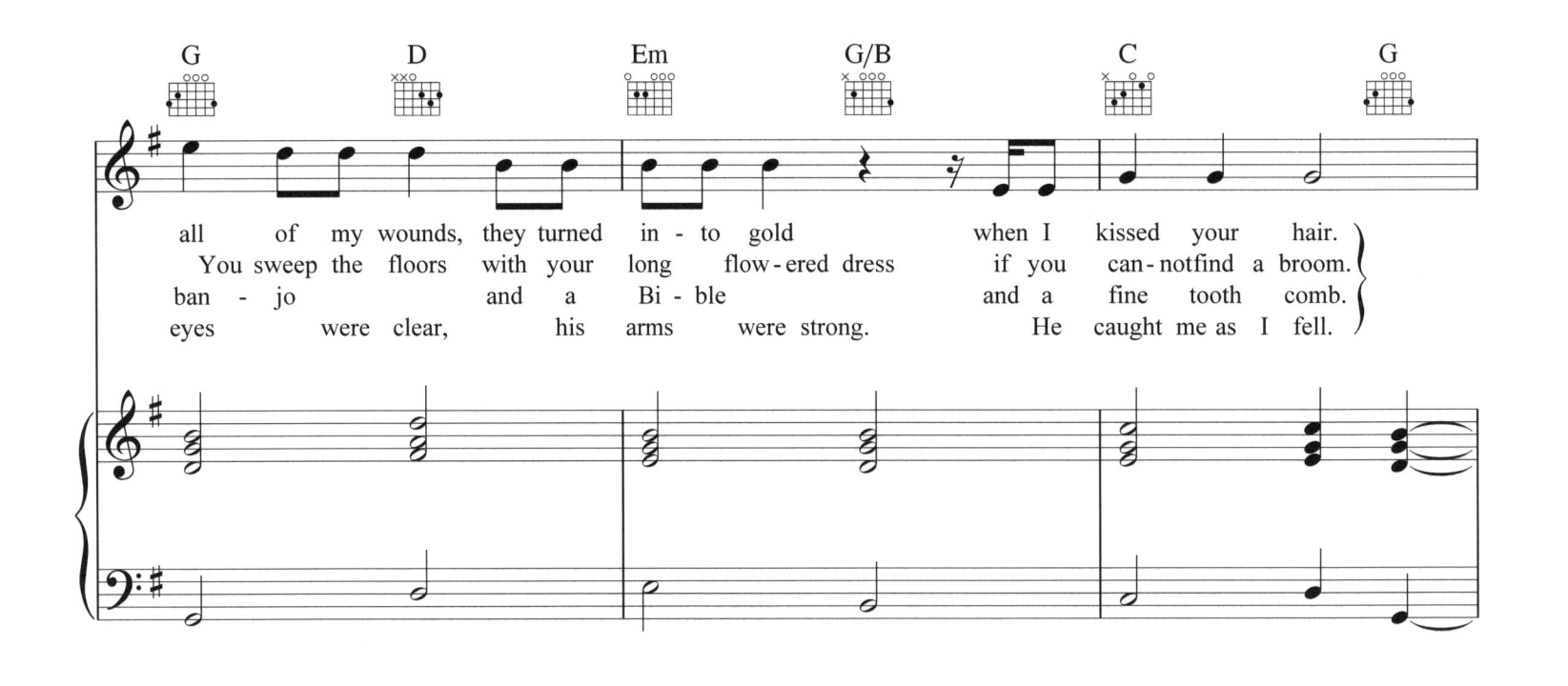

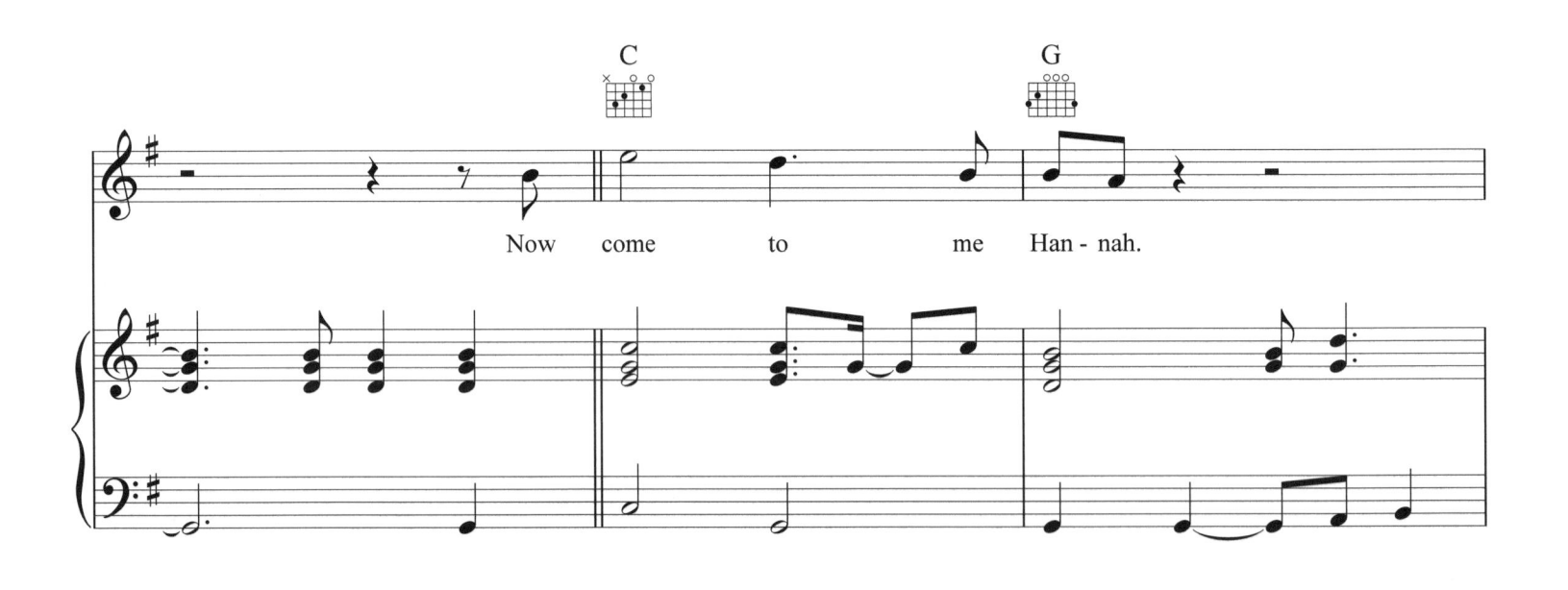

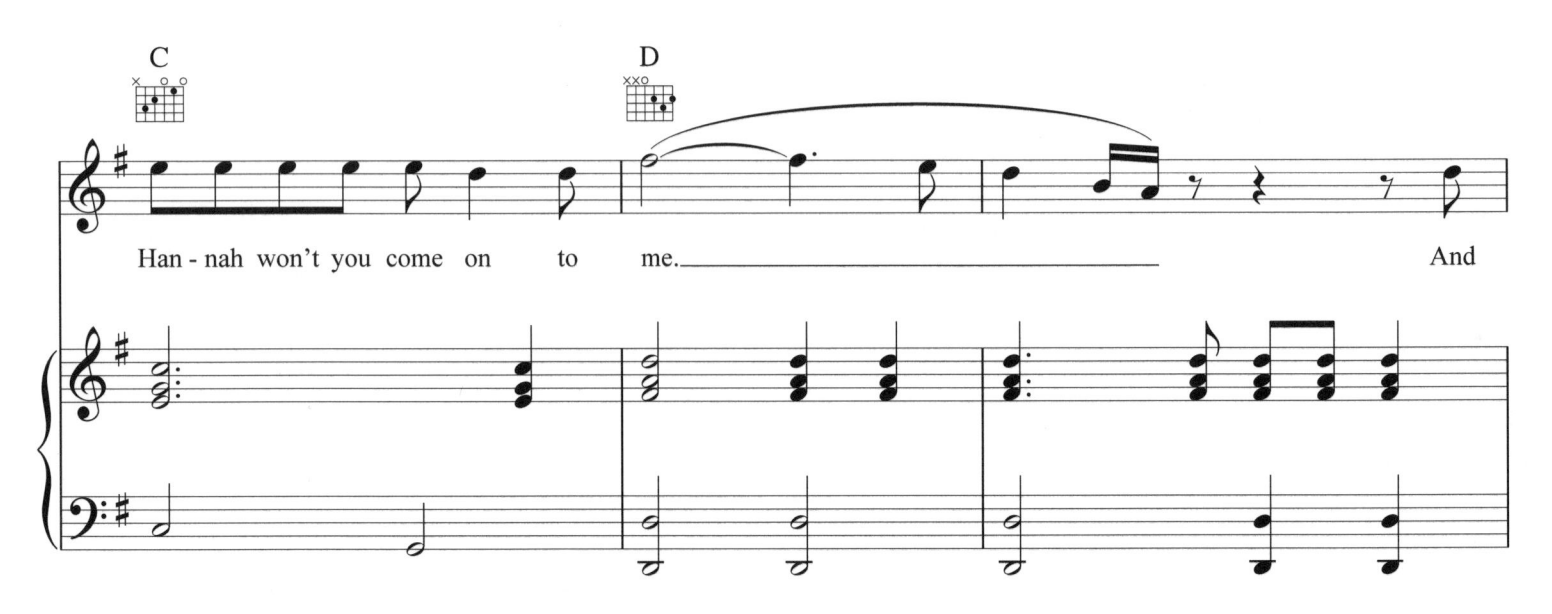

| G | D | Em | G/B | C | G |

all of my wounds, they turned in-to gold when I kissed your hair.
You sweep the floors with your long flow-ered dress if you can-not find a broom.
ban - jo and a Bi - ble and a fine tooth comb.
eyes were clear, his arms were strong. He caught me as I fell.

| C | G |

Now come to me Han - nah.

| C | D |

Han - nah won't you come on to me. And

1, 2.
G D/F♯ C/E G/D D C
I'll lay down this bot - tle of wine if you'll just be kind to me.
3, 4.
D C G C
just be kind to me. Now, I'd walk one mile on just
G C G/B Am
To Coda
bro - ken glass to fall down at your feet.
G D C
Mm, Han - nah, you're the queen of the street.
Violin

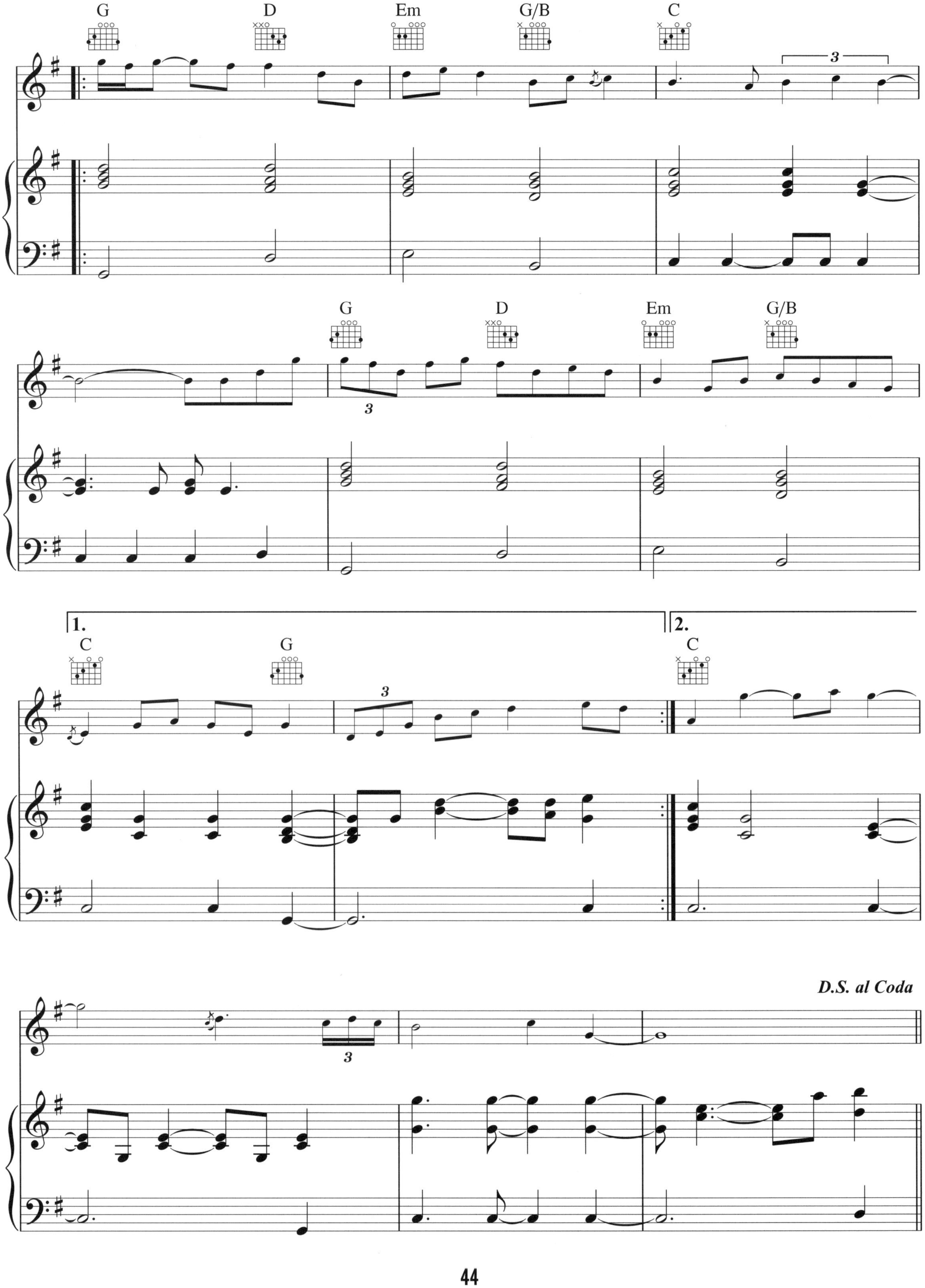
G
D
Em
G/B
C
3
G
D
Em
G/B
3
1.
C
G
3
2.
C
D.S. al Coda
3

Mm,_____ Han - nah,____ you're the queen of the street.

The queen of the street._____

Violin

All The Wild Horses

Words & Music by Ray LaMontagne

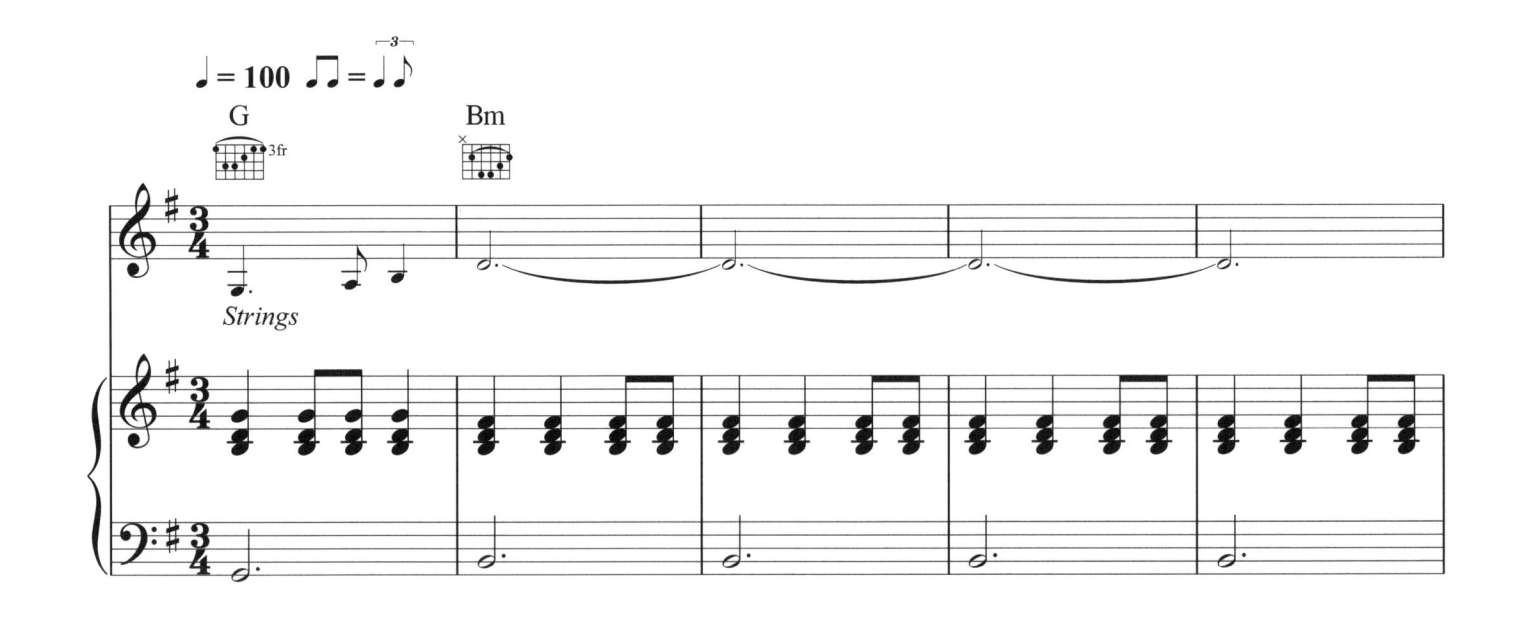

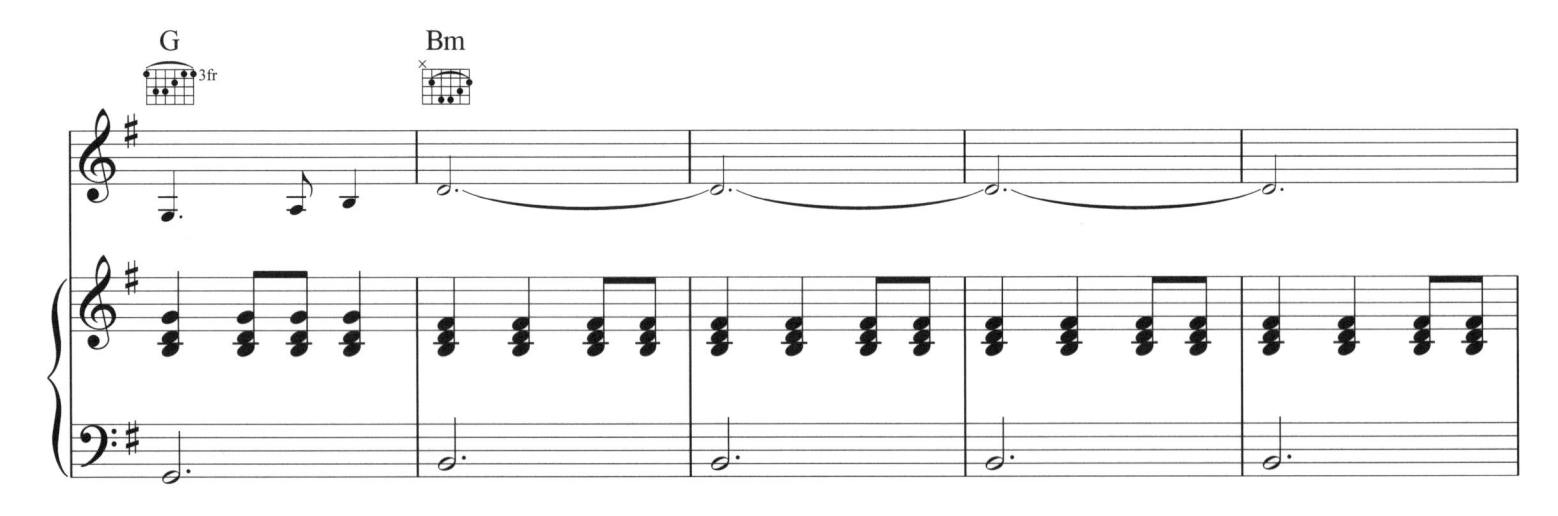

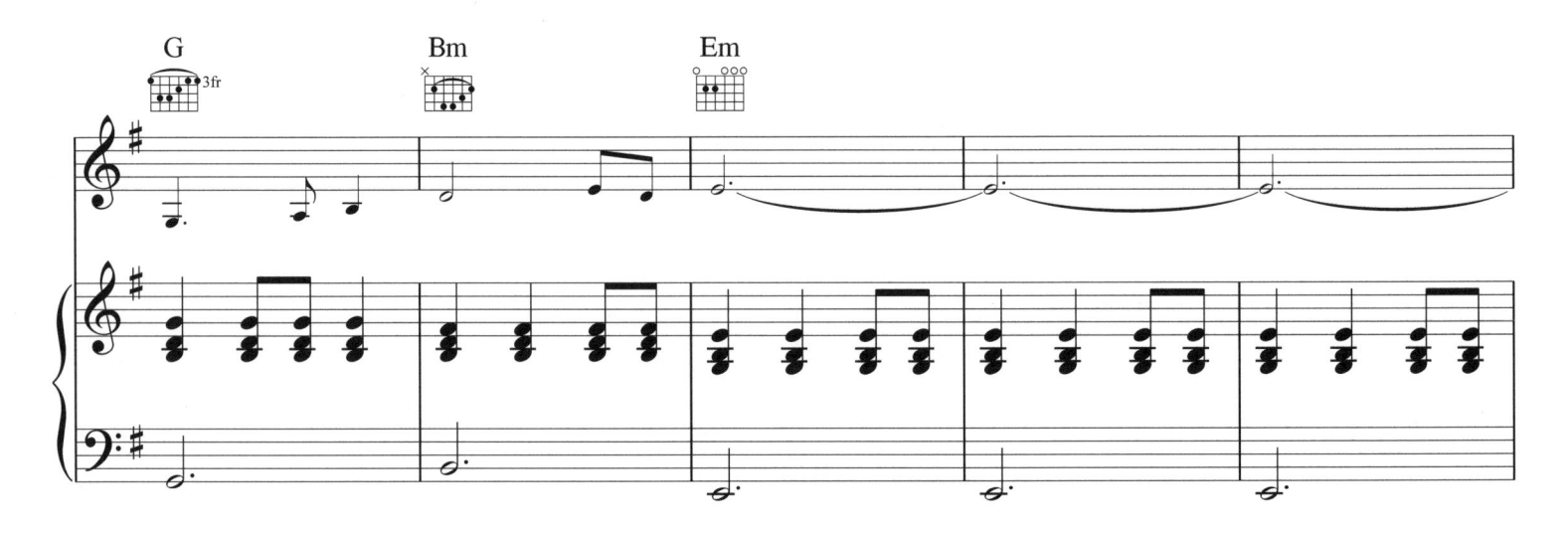

All the wild hors - es.

All the wild hors - es.

Teth - ered with tears in their eyes.

C
G
May no man's touch ev - er tame you.
C
G
May no man's reins ev - er chain you.
D
Em
And may no man's weight ev - er de - frayed your
C
soul.
And as for the clouds,

just let them roll. Roll a-way. Roll a-way. As for the clouds, just let them roll. Roll a-way. Roll a-way. Violin

51

Jolene

Words & Music by Ray LaMontagne

1. Co-caine flame in my blood-stream. Sold my coat when I hit Spok-ane. Bought my-self a hard pack of cig-a-rettes in the
2. Been so long since I seen your face or felt a part of this hu-man race. I've been liv-ing out of this here suit-case for way

© Copyright 2004 Sweet Mary Music, USA.
Chrysalis Music Limited.
All Rights Reserved. International Copyright Secured.

early morning rain. Lately my hands, they don't
_____ too long. A man needs something he can

feel like mine.____ My eyes been stung with dust I'm blind.__
hold on to____ A nine pound hammer or a woman like you.

Held_ you_ in my arms____ one_ time.. Lost you just the same.
Either one of them things____ will_ do.____

Jo-lene,____ I ain't a-bout to go

straight.___ It's too late.___ I found___ my-self___ face down in the ditch, booze___ in my hair,___ blood on my lips. A pic-ture of you___ hold-ing a pic-ture of me___ in the pock-et of my___ blue jeans. Still don't know what love___

C
Em
G
means.
Still don't know what love
C
G/B
Am
C
G/B
Am
means.
Jo - lene.
G
C
G/B
Am
To Coda
La la la la la la la.
Jo - lene.
G
C/G
G
C/G

La la la la la la la. Jo-lene.